D1515019

Faith Wick
Doll Maker Extraordinaire

by Helen Bullard

Ruffles. Photograph by Keith Pollister.

COVER ILLUSTRATION: *Nast Santa* with *Buttons* and *Bows.* Photograph by Keith Pollister.

Published by HOBBY HOUSE PRESS, INC.
Cumberland, Maryland 21502

The Necromancer, The Sorcerer and *The Wizard. Photograph by Keith Pollister.*

Additional copies of this book may be purchased at $12.95
from
HOBBY HOUSE PRESS, INC.
900 Frederick Street
Cumberland, Maryland 21502
or from your favorite bookstore or dealer.
Please add $1.75 per copy postage.

Elfie. Photograph by Keith Pollister.

Fashionable Ladies. Photograph by Keith Pollister.

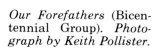*Our Forefathers* (Bicentennial Group). *Photograph by Keith Pollister.*

4

Wicket Witch. Photograph by Mike Illies.

Pom-Pom (white costume) and Tom-Tom (red costume). Photograph by Keith Pollister.

Holiday Children. Photograph by Keith Pollister.

Contents

I. Beginnings, Teaching, Marriage, Children....13

II. The Theme Park. Educating Mama............19

III. First Original Dolls.................................29

IV. Wicket Originals, Inc. 39

V. Commercial Designs 49

VI. New House and New Plans 91

Introduction

An hour's flight from Minneapolis, Minnesota, on a nice little "puddle-jumper" and you land in Grand Rapids, Minnesota, a town near the Minnesota Iron Range. Faith Wick was born in Buhl, one of the little towns on the Range and grew up to teach school there. It is beautiful rolling country and except during its punishing winters, you can drive its long, uncrowded roads and fish its creeks and rivers — and the glorious Mississippi. The source of this noblest of our rivers is in the northern part of the state — a puddle of a lake bearing the Indian name "Itasca." Faith and Mel took me there and we waded in the headwaters.

Faith and Mel have spent their lives here and created a saga of their own that could compete with any of the Norse ones. The saga is rapidly getting out of control. No, they have not built a 15-room house with the dining room cantilevered over the Mississippi River. No, she has not just signed a contract to design 50 dolls for a foreign manufacturer. No, she is not quitting designing.

Even so, her story is wild and woolly — and Faith, herself, admits that it is pretty sensational although, so she says, it is entirely without VIOLENCE!

Still, Faith is violently alive. She turns out a volume of work possible only to a hard-driving person with places to go and things to do in endless listings.

Faith Wick and some of her creations.

Helen Bullard (left) and Faith Wick at Itasca Creek, 1982.

8

Clowns. *Photograph by Keith Pollister.*

Faith Wick.

Jester. Photograph by Keith Pollister.

Jazz Man. Photograph by Keith Pollister.

Anchors Aweigh Boy and Girl, Party Time Boy and Girl, Scarecrow and Clown. Photograph by Keith Pollister.

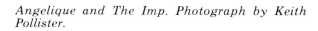
Angelique and The Imp. Photograph by Keith Pollister.

Bing. Photograph by Keith Pollister.

Jolly Old Elf. Photograph by Keith Pollister.

Blue Indigo. Photograph by Keith Pollister.

Traditional Magician. *Photograph by Mike Illies.*

Bag Lady. Photograph by Keith Pollister.

Three Maids, 1776, 1876 and *1976. Photograph by Mike Illies.*

St. Ives with Bagpipes. *Photograph by Keith Pollister.*

Bob Cratchit, Scrooge and *Tiny Tim* (Christmas Carol). *Photograph by Keith Pollister.*

I.
Beginnings, Teaching, Marriage, Children

Faith Wick was born on Minnesota's Iron Range not far from the source of the Mississippi River. Her mother and father were nurse and doctor in the little mining town which was full of immigrant workers in strange clothes — women in shawls and men in pantaloons and soft caps. Their ways were strange and their problems often difficult to understand.

She spent much time until she was eight or nine with her little brother, Bruce, both being under the care of their grandmother. Her father — an eye, ear, nose and throat specialist — was ill and hospitalized while her mother supported the family. Faith and her brother were devoted to the book, *Hans Brinker*, because Hans and his family were waiting for his father to get well.

"As a very young child," says Faith, "I engaged in many attention-getting types of behavior. In second grade I tore up the report card of the best looking boy in the class because he wouldn't pay any attention to me. I spent much time in the grades drawing my own cartoons and a continuing series of story-pictures that became small books. I wrote plays and poetry — always illustrated — and

took dancing and acrobatic lessons from Tony Charmoli who is now one of Hollywood's most famous choreographers." (She can still stand on her head in good form.)

"Mother could not fix my hair in the long curls she wanted me to have, so I went to the beauty parlor every Saturday and also had a manicure to help me quit biting my nails! I loved to watch how ladies had perms and cuts and what they wore. Mother read aloud daily — mostly nursery rhymes and fairy tales. And Grandma made me lovely dresses and things and hand knit sweaters.

"Music played an important part in my early childhood. Mother was an accomplished pianist and would play the piano while my brother and I sang. We also took piano lessons. Our friend, Uncle Bill, a businessman, would come dressed in a tux and white silk shirt. He danced to the music with a gowned mannequin called 'Zelda' attached to his feet while 'Aunt Inez,' his wife, and we would dance wildly together while Mother played the piano.

"I was a very domineering child and remember having to bribe children to play with me. I always wanted to plan the activities which were acting out a story I had heard of,

Faith Wick, age three months.

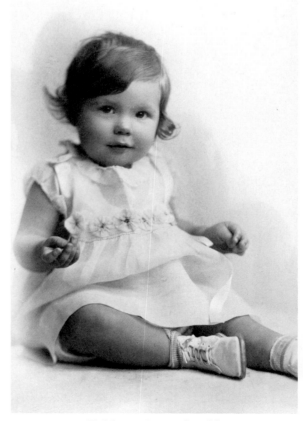

Faith at 18 months old.

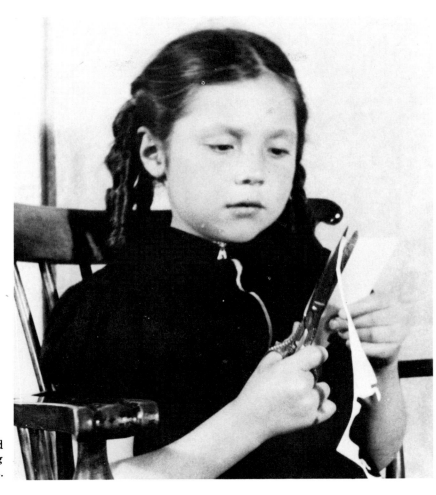

Seven-year-old
Faith cutting
paper dolls.

Faith created activities in her childhood with her
dolls, mimicking things her mother did in the adult
world.

or one I was making up. I wanted all the major
roles. What I really liked were fairy tales in
which I could be the hero and the heroine and
the wicked witch all at once. Needless to say, I
was not a popular child, but I kept trying to
win approval in every way I could. I never got
into serious trouble.

"My junior high school days, as I see them
now, had much to do with my adult career in
sculpting and designing. When I was about 12
I was finally allowed some freedom away
from my own yard, and alone. With my
bicycle I explored abandoned iron pits which
were filled with water and usually dangerous
and I discovered the woods and hills at close
range. I could see for myself wonders which
had only been part of my make-believe. During
high school I had lots of boyfriends and went
with a group of girls that I was comfortable
with but never felt truly a part of. They
laughed a lot and I could never figure out why.
And when I thought something was funny,
they did not know why I was laughing."

Recently, when Faith searched old albums
for early photographs, she was astonished to

discover that in most of them she was holding or playing with a doll. She had made her own dolls very early, white cloth stuffed with cotton with painted or crudely stitched features.

"After high school," Faith confesses, "my mother and her six brothers tried to bribe me to go to college, but I was rebellious about following the accepted family pattern and decided to go to work in a shirt factory. After a year of this mindless activity I was more than happy to go to college. My two-year degree for teaching kindergarten gave me the chance to have the same kind of elaborate doll arrangements for the children which I had made for myself as a little girl who played alone much of the time in her large outdoor playhouse. Now, as a kindergarten teacher, I could have a wonderful doll corner for the often underprivileged children whom I was teaching. I introduced them to a fairy-tale world of fancy circuses and farms with animals known only in fantasies."

Gives Shower for New Doll

Miss Fuller and the children of the kindergarten class entertained at a shower given in honor of their new doll. Mothers of the children were invited and refreshments were served. The doll received many lovely gifts. Out of town guests were R. J. Scofield and Miss Lavona Jasper.

Even in her teaching activities Faith Wick used dolls to teach children social amenities.

Faith, age 20, on Bemidji State College campus, posing with her Effanbee doll.

Each doll had her own baby book, her own fingerprints (Faith's), locks of her hair (also Faith's) to give for keepsakes, and even a trunkful of costumes for her own make-believe. Faith was in her element.

She was also being courted by handsome, shrewd, pink-cheeked and tolerant Melvin Wick, a young miner who worked with a gang of craftsmen who, on receipt of an order from U.S. Steel (their company) for so many car-loads of iron ore, got it out and shipped it without bosses, job tickets or any outside supervision.

Presently, Mel and Faith were married and in a few years produced four children. Faith lost no year of teaching during this period and when the last child was still a nursing baby, she began her famous saga of eight summers of finishing her education. Another adventure, however, came first.

Faith during her first teaching position changed the decor of her desk monthly.

Faith and Mel Wick on their wedding day.

II.
The Theme Park.
Educating Mama

Faith Wick's workshop at Fairyland Park.

The Wick sense of adventure must have been operating overtime when they had a chance to buy a broken-down "theme park" in 1960. "Fairyland Park" was a children's fantasy with life-size figures in cement in an outdoor setting along a path in a natural woodland. The Wick family lived in a little fairy-tale French-style cottage in the park and the children played in the Old Woman's Shoe! (What marvelous stories those children can tell their own children some day!)

"I continued to teach," says Faith, "and Mel and I learned to handle the cement for the figures." Faith worked at repairing the broken figures and then making new ones. It was not long before she, and others, saw that her figures were better than the originals.

"The most loved — and feared — character in the park," Faith recalls, "was the Wicked Witch. Her eyes glowed in the dark and I made a witch-like cackling voice recording for her. The children feared she was alive. To this day witches are my favorite subjects. They may stem from those old European grandmothers I was afraid of and yet fascinated by

in the little mining towns I grew up in. They were toothless and bent, wore long black clothes and spoke in strange languages.

"When the children were young I went back to college every summer — for eight summers — starting with a nursing baby, a three- and a four-year-old, a six-year-old and a young baby-sitter. With no car! We lived in an unfurnished big old house. One child slept in the buggy, one in the bathtub and the rest of us on cots. We had a card table and four chairs and that was it. We went to the laundromat with the baby in a stroller, dirty clothes in the buggy (no Pampers as yet), one child in a harness tied to the buggy and one holding the hand of the baby-sitter as she pushed the baby in the stroller; and one independent six-year-old."

The children slept in places like the University of Minnesota library captain's chairs while Faith did research. With details rearranged to suit the changing ages of the supporting players, this performance went on for eight summers. Also, the show was put on at eight different colleges so that Faith could get

Mary Had a Little Lamb, Fairyland Park, Marble, Minnesota.

Fairyland Park.

the courses she needed to obtain a special degree which was then new and not generally available.

Thus, Faith's (that name must surely have been given to her for some reason!) *modus operandi* during those eight years while this educating was going on was:

September through May: School teaching.

May and half of June: Repainting "Fairy-land Park" figures and creating new ones.

Mid June to September: Faith and the kids went to college and Mel tended the park after his daily working hours in the mine. A hired woman minded the park while he was at work.

Faith took the kids and went to college every summer for eight years. She achieved a B.S. and a Master's in Education from St. Cloud State College and the University of Minnesota.

After this legendary hegira ("Obstacle Course," "Trial by the Fates," and so forth) was finished, Faith, with her precious new sheepskin clutched firmly in her two hands (the children could now walk alone), reached her objective of Director of a county school for mentally retarded children and adults, and a substantial increase in salary.

With more time and money at her disposal (and no summer studying), she began collecting and costuming dolls. Not one here and two there, however, (as you or I might do) but a grand total of nearly 500 antique porcelain dolls. She loved researching, cataloging and costuming them. She was still teaching school and she and Mel were still operating "Fairy-land Park." Mel had been both groundskeeper and general manager of the park all along and he grew beautiful flowers in it every year. With the help of a competent housekeeper, they kept everything going. They lived there for 15 years.

Presently, since the children needed a bigger senior high school, Faith and Mel decided to move to the closest large town. They sold "Fairyland Park" and the vast collection of newly-costumed and cataloged dolls in order to buy an 18-room house in the town of Grand Rapids, Minnesota, and an A-frame cabin on the Mississippi at Cohasset for summer fun.

There were three pianos in the house. Faith's mother also had an apartment there. (Please note that there is usually a wild corner in every family scene!)

Fairyland Park.

Fairyland Park.

Fairyland Park.

Fairyland Park.

Fairyland Park.

Faith Wick and her first sculpture, Maria Sanford,
in front of Sanford Hall, Bemidji State College,
Bemidji, Minnesota.

Old Mother Hubbard.

Alice

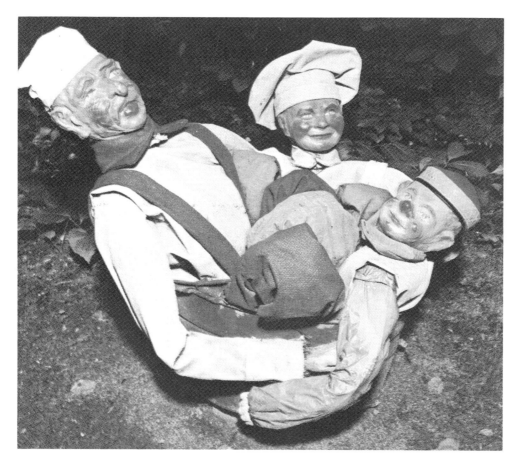

Rub-a-Dub-Dub,
Three Men in a Tub.

Little Jack Horner.

III.
First Original Dolls

"After we sold out in 1975 and moved to Grand Rapids, I missed having the 500 antique dolls to study and costume as well as the sculpting and creating of the large people figures and animals for the park. Because the modeling of the figures had 'come easy,' I began to create small people figures using techniques similar to those I had developed in making the large figures.

"I sculpted in clay, later in Polyform, and made a rubber mold, then poured plaster in the mold, imbedding a wire armature within it. Then I painted the plaster head with acrylics, slipped a body suit over the wire armature and stuffed it with polyester fiberfill. Then I costumed and wigged the doll. Later on, I dipped the dolls in wax before wigging and dressing them. This gave them a soft natural look.

"Doll making was the most fascinating thing I had ever done. It combined all the things I love to do: research, organization, creating, sculpting, costuming and painting; and later, organizing my own production operation and hitting the road to sell the dolls.

"It took a little while to develop a stock of dolls, but in the summer of 1973 (and during the next five summers) I traveled on the Greyhound bus (99 days for $99) with a ticket for me and one for the child who went with me (they took turns; my mother, too). This travel was undertaken to cover the various doll shows being given across the country. We looked like tramps while traveling, but put on our good clothes — and often costumes — for the shows.

"I created so many one-of-a-kind dolls during this early period that I cannot remember them except in categories; such as fantasies, historical characters, humorous characters, Christmas and fairy tale — favorites, clowns and children. All were copyrighted with the date and Faith Wick. These were the dolls I took with me to sell on my trips to shows. One day the Greyhound Bus Company lost my luggage on a trip to Sioux Falls, South Dakota. I was scheduled to speak on my cloth doll patterns and the development of my sculptured dolls before a large audience there.

"Not only was I dressed in my serviceable traveling costume of plaid shirt, bib overalls, sneakers and a cloth newsboy cap, but I was totally out of exhibit materials. All I had was a plastic pail of clay which I always carried onto the bus so as to be able to work instead of sit.

"Several hundred interested doll collectors and no program!

"So I gave an unscheduled, unrehearsed step-by-step lecture on the art of sculpting a doll — something I had been doing for years, but never dreamed of teaching someone else to do. My professional knowledge of how to reduce a process to simple, organized teaching for retarded people now stood me in good stead. I quickly created a doll head and hands before the eyes of the fascinated watchers, and thus began my teaching career in sculpting original dolls.

"So for a few years I taught classes in doll making all summer in many states."

In 1976, Faith was elected to membership in the National Institute of American Doll Artists, the first and very prestigious artists-in-dolls organization. Among her earlier dolls bearing the NIADA label are: *Iron Miner, Mexican Band, Jason, Jack Frost, Black Doctor* and *Old Lady in the Park.*

By this time she had discovered a new plastic clay which could be oven-fired and painted. This became her medium. (The reason she had never worked in porcelain was her asthma, which made it impossible.)

She still took to the road to sell her dolls at the leading doll shows around the country. Then she would have to go home and build up a stock before she could go out again. It did

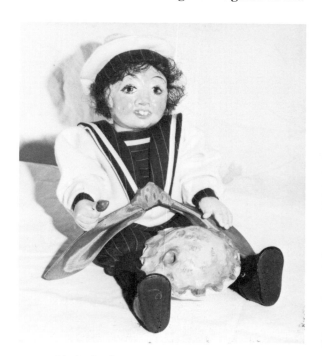

Little Jack Horner, 1972. Polyform.

Original work in Polyform by Faith Wick, 1973.

not take her long to figure that she had an endless market out there and that she was treating it like a Sunday hobby.

What should she do?

"The reason I left my fine steady job was that the doll business presented a career that had so many more interesting facets than I could envision in my well-paying, tenured teaching job. I liked the idea of being free of boards, free of staying in one building for eight hours, free to meet people other than educators, free to create things with my hands, free to meet the challenge of earning a living when you were not on a salary and knew what your income would be, and also free to have the working hours of my own choice, be they ever so much longer than a 40 to 50-hour week.

"The challenge of trying the unknown was so right at this time. I had had a taste of it by doing it on weekends and a bit in the summer, so I had some idea of what could be done with the idea. My children were old enough to enjoy the experiment, which meant travel with me which added a new dimension to their lives. We had not done much traveling with them as young children from our somewhat remote northern home, partly because of having to care for the Park and having to go to summer school all those years.

"I longed for a new lifestyle with none of the elements that I suddenly found terribly confining, and I could do it without leaving everything that was dear to me. I included the family in as much of the experience as they wished to share, and still left room for their development of their own ideas. The decision took sensitivity to the needs of all and a lot of very hard work."

Hansel and *Gretel*, 1974. NIADA. Polyform.

Artist Clown, Faith Wick's first doll in porcelain, 1973.

The *Black Doctor*, made by Faith Wick to honor her father, a doctor. Presented to and accepted by NIADA's Standards Committee, 1976. Polyform.

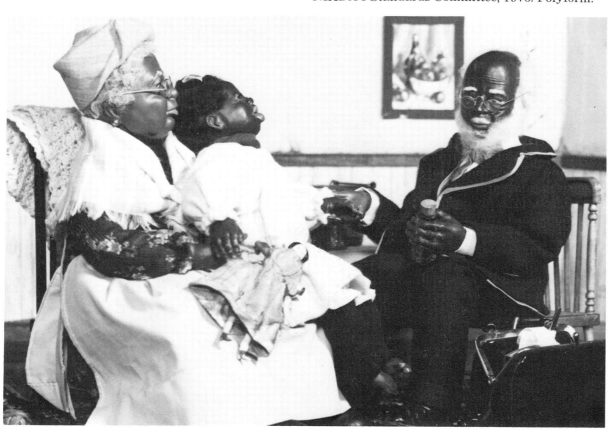

First Prize at the Fair, 1977. NIADA. Polyform.

Old Lady in the Park of Polyform and wax, 1978. NIADA.

Fiddler, 1978. NIADA, Polyform.

Baby's First Skates, 1978. NIADA. Polyform.

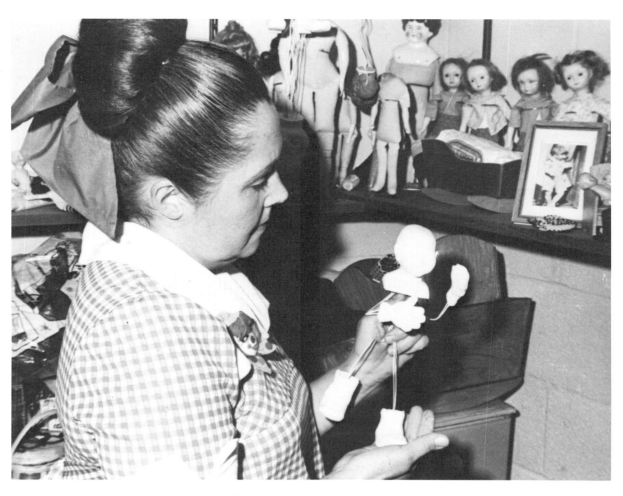

Faith Wick holding *Artist Clown.*

Grandma Moses, 1978.
NIADA. Polyform.

Mexican Band,
1979. NIADA.
Polyform.

Iron Miner, 1979. NIADA. Polyform.

Jack Frost, 1979. NIADA. Polyform.

Jason, 1979. NIADA. Polyform.

Scott Joplin, 1980. NIADA. Polyform.

IV.
Wicket Originals, Inc.

Faith resigned her safe, well-paying job and set up "Wicket Originals, Inc." as a cottage industry. The dolls produced would be fine handmade porcelain duplicates of her designs, but she would not have to perform each of the numerous and tedious tasks. She could supervise the entire operation.

Wick created the designs; she sculptured, discussed the painting with porcelain artisans, and dressed the prototype; and then she assigned the various different types of work with patterns and specific instructions to the 60 or 70 different craftsmen who fabricated the dolls; molding, casting and finishing the porcelain parts; painting the faces, wigging the heads, making the bodies and dressing the finished dolls with the clothing made by the dressmakers.

The usual limit for each edition was 100 dolls. Some of the designs, however, were made in smaller quantities; a few in larger.

The professional craftsmen who constituted the staff of this intricate organization worked at home in various parts of the country. Most of them Faith had met on her travels to shows. It was, of course, due partly to her wide acquaintance with these fabricators that she was emboldened to set up such a complex "spread-out factory" for the production of fine porcelain dolls. In 1979, she bought a big old house to use just for

Wicket Originals: stock and operations. It was on the shore of Forest Lake and looked a perfect doll house.

How did she maintain high quality under such complex conditions? It was mostly accomplished by first choosing professional craftsmen. She controlled quality by not paying for work that was not up to specifications. This happened rarely and there was no breakage in transit. Faith says, "We saw every doll that was shipped and really had very few problems. I already had had experience in my former career with hiring people. I knew what I wanted and was able to make my specifications clear and simple."

It was not long before she started working with manufacturers' representatives (1979) and selling in various merchandise marts. After several months she decided to sign up with a single representative, Davis-Grabowski, based in Miami, Florida.

Under each of these arrangements she was obliged to spend a lot of time on the road. The selling pattern started with her personal appearance at various stores. The store would purchase at least ten Wicket Originals and then she would make up a circuit from the many invitations that came to her for these personal promotions, and she had to be careful not to book too many appearances and wear herself out. The usual routine was a

Joanne   Jeanette   Janice   Judith

Fashion Ladies in Fancy Dress from the Wicket Originals catalog.

OPPOSITE PAGE: American Heritage collection from the Wicket Originals catalog.

press party, followed by a special cocktail party for dignitaries. Then during the next two days would come the sales and autograph signing by Faith. She soon discovered that when she appeared in special costumes to create an effect, the sales were better.

"I have been making costumes," she wrote, "the more theatrical I am, the better 'my public' remembers me...and they think it is fun to see a little fat lady dressed up like a witch — or whatever.

"Mel is out of a job because U. S. Steel has shut down his mine. Just before Christmas he helped to weld the doors shut," Faith wrote me in 1980. "He is finding a niche for himself in the doll business as purchasing agent and money manager and he's very good at it. He should make the business a real paying proposition. I am glad to be designing and not minding all the details...I have just put out my first catalog (January, 1980) with 60 designs made by Wicket Originals, Inc. and plan to put one out every January and June."

In July 1982, Faith sold one each of her "Wicket Originals" (now numbering some 500 designs), plus several NIADA dolls from her collection to a collector who was thinking of a museum. The price was $100,000.

"My problem with Wicket Originals," wrote Faith in a rare letter, "was that I played too many parts: designer, sculptor and business manager. I knew everyone's role and had to keep track of all parts at all times (without a computer!). I decided that my business would have to go to a more automatic method of manufacture or stop. I personally was not interested in running a factory, so I opted to be a designer only."

Thus it was that in 1982, although Wicket Originals, Inc. was producing considerable profit, this successful cottage industry was closed down. The operation had grown so large that it was a kind of madness to keep the records of so many scattered workers.

Many editions of 100 have already been sold out. In 1982, retail prices of this series of dolls ranged from $300 to $1500. (The latter price was for *Queen Victoria "Wicktoria".*)

The corporation — Wicket Originals, Inc. — lives on, as the design operation in which Wick is engaged. It is her private designing studio in which she is the designer. Even in this reduced responsibility, her days are more than comfortably filled with designing and public appearances.

Her son, Tim, and his artist wife, Susan, and other gifted artisans develop the prototypes from her sculptures, body and clothing designs which she then offers to certain manufacturers.

Limited production and elegant quality appeal to a discriminating clientele.

American Heritage

Patrick Henry
Aaron Burr
Alexander Hamilton
George Washington in uniform
Benjamin Franklin
James Madison
Thomas Jefferson
Martha Washington
George Washington in fancy dress
Betsy Ross
Dolley Madison

Katie's Kids

Little Bunny Boy

Little Mouse Boy

Pattie and Her Poodle

Little Bear Boy

Little Bunny Girl

Little Bear Girl

Debbie

Donnie

Katie the Clown

Bunny Rabbit

Little Mouse Girl

Sunbonnet Sue

Overall Sam

Katie's Kids collection from the Wicket Originals catalog.

Special Events collection from the Wicket Originals catalog.

Special Events

Mr. Wanderful

Bing, the Clown

Edward, Playing Clown

Hobo, Jr. the Clown

The Candy Man

Graduation Girl

Graduation Boy

Baby Jester

Patches - the Clown

Wicket Original Designs

Colonel Topper, Auctioneer
Mrs. Wiggs of the Cabbage Patch
Wicket Witch
Maid of 1776
Maid of 1876
Maid of 1976
Male Gnome (Gnils)
Female Gnome (Gnina)
Goblinfolk Male
Goblinfolk Female
Goblin King
Goblin Queen
Leprechaun
Brownie
Traditional Santa
Butch
Betsy
Peter
Polly
Pedlar Woman
Pom-Pom
Scarecrow
Fisherboy
Eskimo
Cowboy
Hearth Witch
Chimney Sweep
Three Little Pigs (straw)
Three Little Pigs (sticks)
Three Little Pigs (bricks)
Christmas Fairy
Tooth Fairy
St. Nick
Colonial Lady
Colonial Man
Florence Nightingale
Abraham Lincoln (two sizes)
Mary Todd Lincoln (two sizes)
Gerald Ford
George Washington
Martha Washington
Penelope (white face)
Pearce
Penelope (pink face)
Penelope (masked)
Penelope in Tuxedo
Tiny Tim
Bob Cratchit
Mini Santa
Mini Mrs. Santa

Mini Red Elf
Mini Green Elf
Elf (formerly Abram's Gnome)
Mini Grandfather
Mini Grandmother
Mini Grandson
Mini Granddaughter
Mini Grandchild
Baby Clown with Balloons
Jester
Traditional Magician
Tree Witch
Flapper Fanny
Dapper Dan
Billy Bum
Peter Piper and His Pickled Peppers
Artist Clown
Mini Witch (black shoes)
Mini Witch (red shoes)
Mini Witch with Basket
Casey, the Baby Clown
Easter Boy
Easter Boy (porcelain hair)
Mrs. Claus
Mr. Claus
Great Big Santa Claus
Pied Piper of Hamlin
Folk Santa Papa
Folk Santa Mama
Cinderella/Prince/Step-mother/Godmother
Maskmaker
Delilah
Samson
Merlin, the Magician
Necromancer
Scrooge
Valentine Girl
Valentine Girl (porcelain hair)
Easter Girl
Easter Girl (porcelain hair)
Fourth of July
Fourth of July (porcelain hair)
Christmas Angel
Christmas Angel (porcelain hair)
Pilgrim Boy
Pilgrim Boy (porcelain hair)

Pilgrim Girl
Pilgrim Girl (porcelain hair)
Halloween Witch
Halloween Witch (porcelain hair)
Halloween Devil
Halloween Devil (porcelain hair)
Christmas Clown
Christmas Clown (porcelain hair)
Happy Birthday Clown
Happy Birthday Clown (porcelain hair)
Baby Bunny (larger skull/open mouth)
Baby Bunny (closed mouth)
Baby Bear (open mouth)
Baby Bear (closed mouth)
Tree Troll
Apple Annie
Apple Annie (apples on cheeks)
Baby Seth (closed eyes)
Baby Seth (open eyes)
Baby Sara with Curl (closed eyes)
Baby Sara (open eyes)
Edward as Clown (patriotic)
Edwinna as Bride
Elizabeth as Clown (patriotic)
Elizabeth in Pink
Elizabeth in Brown
Heartley
Queen Bee
Lady Bug
Berry Red Dwarf
Moss Green Dwarf
Dusty Rose Dwarf
Bluejay Blue Dwarf
Raven Black Dwarf
Leaf Rust Dwarf
Fawn Brown Dwarf
Snow White
Old Woman in the Shoe
Toymaker
Toymaker's Wife
Tom Tom, the Clown
Mr. Know-It-All
Jolly Old Elf (Long John Santa)
Flapper Franny

Father Christmas with Santa
  Mask
Great Big Clown
Billy Bum (Effanbee)
Swamp Witch
Swamp Bride
Swamp Bridesmaid
Ruthie in the Rain
Richie in the Rain
Debbie (Balos)
Donnie (Balos)
Donnie Lee
Debbie Lou
Bing, the Fashion Clown
Bing, the Fashion Clown
  (Silvestri)
Blue Indigo Clown with Mask
Hobo Clown
Hobo Clown, Jr.
St. Patrick Boy
St. Patrick Boy (porcelain
  head)
Little Sultan
Cathy
Carl
Woodland Wizard
Wooden Indian (female and
  male)
Angelique
Bows (Little Apple's Com-
  panion, Apple Lil)
Troll (male and female)
Troll (gnome baby boy and
  girl)
Buttons (Li'l Apple)
Jean
Joan
June
Jane
Jeanette
Joanne
Judith
Janice
Hunter
Papa's Boy
Mama's Boy
Peg O'My Heart
Peg O'My Heart
Prince
Pauper
Sammy
Lila
Buttons, Bobby (first model)
Bows, Betty (first model)
Bows (apple cheeks)
Michael John (black)

Melinda Jane (black)
Baby Jester
Harlequin with Hat
Christmas Toddler (girl and
  boy)
Old Woman Market Pedlar
Colonial Maid
Peter in Dr. Denton's (Balos)
Polly in Nightgown (Balos)
Ping
Pong
Gretchen
Gregory
Christmas Elf Man
Christmas Elf Woman
Hunny Bunny
Sonny Snowshoes
Hunny Bear
Saint Ives and Bag Pipes
Nast Santa
Ruffles
Queen Wick-toria
Classic Clown with Mask
Cowgirl Ruthie
Cowboy Richie
Sorcerer
Hansel
Old Man Winter
Gift Giver
Apple for the Teacher
Patty and Her Poodle
Saint Patrick and Harp
Foxy Little Lady
Blue Bows
Brown Bows
Brown Derby
Little Bum Clown
Mr. Mistletoe
Little Miss Dress-Up Playing
  Mommy
Little Miss Dress-Up as
  Patches, the Clown
Elfie
Peter in White (Balos)
Cavalier
Brown Elf
Red Elf
Green Elf
Mr. Pig
Mrs. Pig
Michael
Melinda
Jazzman
Jill as Katie Clown
Jack as Katie Clown
Shoemaker

Shoemaker's Wife
Shoemaker's Elf
Baby Kitten
Baby Mouse
Mob Cap
Mr. Clause in Velvet (with
  sleigh)
Sunday Best
White Fuzz-haired Clown Boy
White Fuzz-haired Clown Girl
Charles
Carolina
Green Goblin
Peggy and Her Peke
Cry Baby Blessing (two sizes)
Amy (country girl)
Andy (country boy)
Bunny Rabbit (real fur)
Sailor Boy (Effanbee)
Sailor Girl (Effanbee)
Party Time Boy (Effanbee)
Party Time Girl (Effanbee)
Clown Boy (Effanbee)
Clown Girl (Effanbee)
Lord Giles
George Washington Clown
Martha Washington Clown
Wee Wicket Witch
Wee Wicket Witch Puppet
Nativity Set (seven men)
Betty Davis
Baby Raggedy Annabelle
Baby Raggedy Andyless
Cruella
Little Vendor Woman
Little Boy Blue (Bruce)
Apple Jack
Charles Lindbergh
Heart-Lequin
Cry Baby Girl
Cry Baby Boy
Cry Baby Bunting
Miniature Cry Baby (Dolls-
  part)
Cry Baby (two sizes — Sil-
  vestri)
Cry Baby (two sizes)
King of Sing a Song of Six-
  pence
Wee Hearth Witch
Street Urchin Girl
Street Urchin Boy
Baby Devil Clown
Margie
Martin
Notion Nanny

Summer Elf
Winter Elf
Spring Elf
Fall Elf
Fairy Elf in Nativity Set (two women)
Teddy, the Bear that Talked Softly
Baby Bruce Clown
Old Woman Notion Pedlar
Old Woman Street Walker
Large Original Li'l Apple (Seth)
Toddler Seth
Toddler Sara
Polly in White (Balos)
Delightful Delilah
Jester (long coat; tie)
Billie
Bonnie
Bobbie
Bunnie
Old Woman Flower Pedlar
Little Black Cat Lady
Little Black Cat Man
Little Black Cat Child
Little White Mouse
Little Grey Country Mouse Lady
Little Grey Country Mouse Man
Little Bunny Lady
Little Bunny Man
Little Bunny Child
Little Bear Lady
Little Bear Man
Little Bear Child
Father Noel (T. S. Wick)
Lady Giles
Hortense
Pinocchio
Pinocchio Puppet
Gepetto
Jolly Santa Ornament (Silvestri)
Mini Emily
Aaron Burr
Alexander Hamilton
Thomas Jefferson
Patrick Henry
Dolley Madison
James Madison
Benjamin Franklin
Betsy Ross
Ruby — Black (Balos)
Rudy — Black (Balos)
Candy Pedlar

Victorian Maid
Baby Sara, Miniature (Balos)
Richie in White (Balos)
Grandma Moses
Bobby in Cowboy Suit
Bobby as Overall Sam
Bobby in White (Balos)
Ruthie in White (Balos)
Bing as Yankee Doodle Dandy
Dapper Danny
Bettie
Mrs. Cratchit
Santa with Molded Beard (Enesco)
Alice (molded hair)
Ruffles in Black
Ruffles in Purple
Strip Poker Pete
Patty and Her Poodle (knits)
Purple Pip
Big Fred (Uncle Sam Clown)
Scandinavian Nisse (knits)
Jester Head on Stick
Know-It-All Clown (red cap and bow tie)
Know-It-All Clown (skull cap)
Know-It-All Clown (red)
Know-It-All Clown (pirate)
Know-It-All Clown (tramp)
Know-It-All Clown (tuxedo)
Know-It-All Clown (silver)
Know-It-All Clown (joker)
Know-It-All Clown (knave of hearts)
Know-It-All Clown (jester)
Blue Indigo Clown Marotte
Queen Alice (Balos)
Queen Alice
Alice Marotte
Alice from the well-known story
Alice Through the Looking Glass
Pip, the Pink Clown (mask)
Pip, Pink Clown Marionette
Falstaff
Axel in Scandinavian Costume
Kim's Wedding Bell
Movie Star Pins
Hulda in Scandinavian Costume
Sweet William, Candy Clown
Ice Princess Ornament (Silvestri)
White Rabbit

White Rabbit (Balos)
White Rabbit in Court
White Rabbit Marotte
White Rabbit in Suit (Dakin)
White Rabbit in Suit (Balos)
Mini Witch Clown
Giant
Groom 1890s
Penelope as Gypsy
Imp Boy
Penny, the Fortune Teller
Yuki
Ichiro
Axel Johnson (two sizes)
Nast Santa II
Scandinavian Elf in Leather, Elvin (Dakin)
Scandinavian Elf
Graduation Girl
Graduation Boy
Groom (Edward)
Groomsman
Best man
Bride (Elizabeth)
Bridesmaid
Maid of Honor
Great Big Hobo
Great Big Farmer
Filipo Doll (Balos)
Filipo Marotte (Balos)
Cavalier Marotte
Mr. Wonderful
Big Bertha, Bag Lady
Bertha, Bag Lady
Pedlar (Effanbee)
Katie, the Klown (red)
Katie, the Klown
Hulda Johnson (two sizes)
Baby Plays Clown (Dollspart)
Mini Eddie
Mini Henry
Mini Henrietta
Sunbonnet Sue
Overall Sam
Gift of Love Ornament (Silvestri)
Snow Girl Ornament (Silvestri)
Mad Hatter (five sizes)
Mad Hatter (Balos)
Mad Hatter Marotte (Balos)
Clyde, the Candyman
Sad Sam, the Balloon Man
Tom Tom, the Piper's Son
Storyteller with Cinderella Masks

Jester Clown Fool
Little Peter Rabbit
Little Flopsie
Little Mopsie
Little Cottontail
Jester Clown (part flesh)
Baby Plays Witch
Baby Plays Hobo
Baby Plays Scarecrow
Baby Plays Mommy
Baby Plays Cinderella
Baby Plays Baseball
Baby Plays Cowboy
Mask for Flossie and Her
  Faces
Witch Hazel
Jessica in Tux
Pig Baby for Alice (Balos)
Wicket Witch of the West
Lily
Duchess from Alice
Duchess from Alice (Balos)
Duchess from Alice Marotte
  (Balos)
Tweedledee and Tweedledum
  (Balos)
Red Skelton as Freddie the
  Freeloader
Red Skelton
March Hare (Balos)
Humpty Dumpty
Humpty Dumpty (Balos)
Mr. Merry Mistletoe
Mad Hatter (molded hair)
Snow Boy with Helmet
  Ornament
Mini Rosemary McCracken
Mini Bonnet Baby Mc-
  Cracken
Santa's Elf
Mini Mrs. McCracken
Ski Bum Clown
Alice, Queen of Hearts
Alice, Queen of Hearts (Balos)
Alice, Queen of Hearts
  Marotte (Balos)
Little Clown Girl
Wee Willie Waukee
Lady Byrd Clown
Jack Frost
Bogey Man
Sandman
Bully Boy
Ten O'Clock Scholar (dunce)
Felicity

Fred Astaire
Littlest Angel Bruce
George Washington Mario-
  nette
Martha Washington Mario-
  nette
Mini Robbie McCracken
Mini Robbie McCracken
  (Silvestri)
Mini Red Wagon Winke
Pioneer Man
Pioneer Woman I
Pioneer Woman II (Dakin)
Colonial Mother (Betsy)
Ass, Brementown Musician
  Doll
Ass, Mechanical
Dog, Brementown Musician
  Doll
Dog, Mechanical
Cat, Brementown Musician
  Doll
Cat, Mechanical
Rooster, Brementown Musi-
  cian Doll
Rooster, Mechanical
Large Clown Ornaments
  (Silvestri)
Victorian Boy (Silvestri)
Eton Boy Ornament
Baby's First Christmas Orn-
  ament
Street Urchin Boy
Street Urchin Girl
Old Fashioned Lady with
  Red Bows Ornament (Sil-
  vestri)
Old Fashioned Lady with
  Lace Ornament (Silvestri)
Old Fashioned Toddler Boy
  and Girl Ornaments (Sil-
  vestri)
Mr. & Mrs. Santa Ornaments
  (Silvestri)
Devil Mask
Witch Mask
Holiday Children
Devil Mask — Maskmaker
  and Thespian (Balos)
Hag Mask — Maskmaker and
  Thespian (Balos)
Bear Mask — Maskmaker
  and Thespian (Balos)
Pig Mask — Maskmaker and
  Thespian (Balos)

Harlequin — Maskmaker and
  Thespian (Balos)
Witch Mask (Wicket Witch)
Pumpkin Accessory —
  Thanksgiving Girl
Jack O'Lantern Accessory —
  Halloween Girl
Thimbles — Opera:
  Carmen
  William Tell
  Pagliaci
  Faust
  Pirates of Penzance
  Madam Butterfly
  (All thimbles for Enesco)
Heart Box Accessory — Val-
  entine Girl (Balos)
Drum Accessory — Fourth of
  July Boy (Balos)
Cornucopia Accessory —
  Thanksgiving Boy
Pipe Accessory — St. Patrick
  Boy
Easter Egg Accessory —
  Easter Girl
Top Accessory — Christmas
  Clown Boy
Gift Box Accessory — Birth-
  day Child
Chocolate Rabbit Accessory
  — Easter Boy
Candle Holder Accessory —
  Christmas Angel
Fly Away Mask — Pip
  Clowns
Alice/Cheshire Cat Chess
  Piece Figurine
Mad Hatter Chess Piece
  Figurine
Card, Red Hood Figurine
Card, Purple Hood Figurine
March Hare/Dormouse
  Figurine
Little Angel — Choir Boy
  Ornaments (Silvestri)
Little Angel — Choir Girl
  Ornament (Silvestri)
Little Chimney Sweep
Santa Mask with Father
  Christmas (Balos)
Pom-Pom Mask
Tom-Tom Mask
Jester Mask with Cavalier or
  Magician
Mini Mr. McCracken

Scandinavian Elf Mask with Elf
Father Christmas Plate, Bell, Mug, Stein and Bear Ornaments (Seeley)
Rhett Butler
Cinderella Mask
Prince Mask
Stepmother Mask
Godmother Mask
Paddy, the Padre Puppet
Little Notion Annie
Kevin, the Christmas Boy
Nutcracker Ornament, Bell — Musical (Enesco)
Pip & Mice — Hamlin Piper Accessory
Mr. Know-It-All in White
Katie, the Klown in Knits
Creche Set — The School Play
Devil Mask, Holiday
Dots (clown)
Young Alice (Dakin)
Father Christmas (Doll-lain)
Eve (Doll-lain)
Epiphany (Doll-lain)
Advent (Doll-lain)
Jack Frost (Doll-lain)
Little Miss Dress-Up (Doll-lain)
Peggy and Her Peke (Doll-lain)
Seth (Doll-lain)
Fancies: Sailor, Newsboy, Skier, Frontier Girl, Baseball Player (black), Clown (Doll-lain)
Pierrot and His Pantin (Doll-lain)
Grandpa in Swing
Grandma in Swing
Cheshire Cat
Merlin Lamp (Enesco)
Merlin Musical (Enesco)
Teddy Bear Clown or Ivan Cinnamon Bear (Balos)
Teddy Bear Santa Claws
Mad Hatter with Closed Mouth (Dakin)
Mini Melanie Wilkes
St. Nick Ornament (Silvestri)
Merlin Ornament (Silvestri)
Large St. Nick
Large Merlin
Jester with Maroon and Pink Ruffles

Jester with Gold, Black and White Short Jacket, Cumberbund
Jester with Maroon and Pink with Bells
Dapper Laurence
Mini Ashley Wilkes
Fool Marotte
Li'l Apple in Overalls with Apple (official convention costume)
Classic Clown Marotte
Classic Clown Jack-in-Box (Enesco)
Holly Pip
Peggy Pekes Pekinese
Pollyanna
Colonial House Maid
Katie Halloween Witch
Betty in Cowgirl Suit
Betty as Sunbonnet Sue
Butch Bum
Gretel
Mini Scarlett O'Hara
Mini Mammy
Mikhail Polar Bear (Balos)
Igor Soldier Bear (Balos)
Mini Mr. O'Hara
Humpty Dumpty (Dollspart)
Bulldog Accessory
Gingerbread Boy Accessory
Puss n' Boots (Dollspart)
Great Grandma Wick
Queen of Hearts (Dollspart)
Pip with Wand, Mechanical
Mini Holly Hobbie
Fool Marotte
Purple Pip in Fur
Cheshire Cat Marotte
Blue Fairy
Navajo Indian
Little Brown Bear
Scandinavian Christmas Elf in Brown
Nast Santa Jack in Box (Enesco)
Circus Jack-in-Box (Enesco)
Lame Fox
Rumplestiltskin
Miller's Daughter
Toy Bear Jack-in-Box (Enesco)
Jester Jack-in-Box (Enesco)
Blind Cat
Eric Rand (Seeley)
Eva Rand (Seeley)

Corinne Rand (Seeley)
Lion Jack-in-Box (Enesco)
Punch Jack-in-Box (Enesco)
Sarah
Grimaldi Clown Jack-in-Box (Enesco)
Rimsky Polar Bear (Balos)
Rudolph Cinnamon Bear (Balos)
Vladimir Brown Bear (Balos)
Ivan Bear Marotte (Balos)
Pedlar Woman (Dakin)
Gift of Love Doll (Silvestri)
Frontier Woman
1890s Bride
Saint Paddy
Brown Barret
Pip Marotte
Greta Rand
Hamilton Rand
Sleepy Bear Doll
Sleepy Bear Marotte
Sleepy Bear Jack-in-Box
Sleepy Bear, Mechanical
Sleepy Bear Button
Old Fashioned Santa
Santa Jack-in-Box (Enesco)
Candy Clown
Bedelia Bag Lady
Snow White Queen Witch
Father Noel, Mechanical
Pedlar (ribbon)
Merry Mistletoe (Silvestri)
Merry Mistletoe Ornament
Twin Baby Boy
Twin Baby Girl
Victorian Skater Man (Silvestri)
Victorian Skater Woman
Jack Frost Ornament (Silvestri)
Baby Bonnet Infant Ornament (Silvestri)
Old Fashioned Girl Doll
Old Fashioned Girl Marotte
Old Fashioned Girl Jack-in-Box
Old Fashioned Girl, Mechanical
Musical Michael (two sizes)
Blue Bell
Old Fashioned Girl Bust Figurine (Enesco)
Cinderella Storyteller
Singing Angel Ornament
Clown Jack Ornament

Santa Jack Ornament
Teddy Bear Jack Ornament
Tree Angel (formal)
Donkey Mask
Cat Caroler Ornament
Dog Caroler Ornament
Rabbit Caroler Ornament
Mouse for Puss 'n Boots
Queen of Hearts (Dakin)
Cinderella
Clown Jack-in-Box Ornament
Santa Jack-in-Box Ornament
Teddy Bear Jack-in-Box
Beauty (Dakin)
Beast Mask (Dakin)
Beast (Dakin)
Puppeteer (Silvestri)
Pinocchio (Silvestri)
Pinocchio No. 2 (Silvestri)
Puppet Theatrical Head (Silvestri)
Little Red Riding Hood
Tuxedo Cat

Wolf — Little Red Riding Hood
Jacque, the Clown
Rose Pip with Stick Mask
Blue Pip with Stick Mask
Fox Hunter
Pirate Puss
Puss 'n Boots
Puss 'n Boots in Brown
Puss 'n Boots in Gray
Bows as Clown
Mid Wife Crisis
Mini Hat Model Head
Geppetto (Silvestri)
Pip as Pagliacci
Pip in Rust/Purple
Pinocchio as Boy with Puppet Mask
Geppetto as Proud Pappa
Snow Girl with Tam
Snow Boy in Brown Suit with Tam
Puss 'n Boots
Snow White (seven sizes)

Old King Cole
Minstrel
Old Salt
Javier, the Jester
Blue Fairy Puppet (silver)
Lame Fox
Blind Cat
Blue Fairy
Punch and Judy Show
Abbie (old fashioned girl)
Abbie Rose
Joyful Jester Figurine (Calatar)
Rabbit Jester
Yodel with Yo-Yo
Bear on Ball Figurine (Enesco)
Bear on Scooter Figurine (Enesco)
Bear Baby with Bottle Figurine (Enesco)
Clown with Hoop Figurine (Enesco)
Cracked Humpty Dumpty

V.
Commercial Designs

Design contracts, which had been increasing steadily, now began to take up all of Wick's time.

1976: Doll-lain Company, Milan, Illinois. "I knew Maureen Malevanko, the owner, from the doll show circuit," says Faith, "and she asked me to design dolls for her to produce in porcelain." She designed the following:

Father Christmas, 20in (51cm); *Eve*, 12in (31cm); *Baby Epiphany*, 7in (18cm); and *Advent*, 10in (25cm). All editions were limited to 100 copies.

Fancies (using same face in variations); all 14in (36cm) and in limited editions of 300.

Also a Clown, Baseball Player (black), Newsboy, Frontier Girl, Skier, Sailor and *Jack Frost*, 20in (51cm); *Pierrot*, 20in (51cm) and *Grandpa and Grandma in Swing*, 18in (46cm). Each limited to 100 copies; porcelain, bearing copyright by Faith Wick.

1979: Convention Heads. These are used as convention and regional meeting souvenirs by the United Federation of Doll Clubs, Inc.

1979: U.F.D.C. Convention, New York, *Li'l Apple*, 16in (41cm). 1500 heads fabricated by Kazue Morai and Muriel Kramer. Edition of 1500 heads. (Portrait of Seth Steven Wick, Wick's grandson.) Bodies were available, also costumes designed by Wick.

Apple Li'l, a little girl designed as *Li'l Apple's* companion, was available, limited to 500 pieces. It was produced by Kazue Morai and handled separately.

1979: Effanbee Doll Corporation, New York. "At a miniature show in Connecticut, I met Roy Raizen, president of Effanbee. He liked my work and asked me to submit a sample. I did and he sent me a contract," writes Faith. "He then made *Party Time Girl, Party Time Boy, Anchors Aweigh Girl* and *Anchors Aweigh Boy*." (Same head and body, adapted.) All Effanbee dolls were made of vinyl. The witches and *Scarecrow* have soft bodies.

Effanbee Doll Corporation
(Craftsmen's Corner)

Name	Size	Years Made
Party Time Girl	16in (41cm)	1979-80
Party Time Boy	16in (41cm)	1979-80
Anchors Aweigh Girl	16in (41cm)	1979-80
Anchors Aweigh Boy	16in (41cm)	1979-80
Clown Girl	16in (41cm)	1980-83
Clown Boy	16in (41cm)	1980-81
Hearth Witch	18in (46cm)	1981-82
Wicket Witch	18in (46cm)	1981-82
Peddler	16in (41cm)	1981-82
Billy Bum	16in (41cm)	1982
Old Fashioned Nast Santa	18in (46cm)	1982-83
Scarecrow	18in (46cm)	1983-84

From the 1979 Effanbee catalog, *Party Time Girl* and *Boy* in their lined velvet costumes and matching berets.

From the 1979 Effanbee catalog, *Anchors Aweigh Boy* and *Girl* in their "crew" cloth sailor costumes with matching hats.

From the 1984 Effanbee catalog, Wick's 18in (46cm) *Scarecrow*.

Faith Wick dolls from Effanbee's "Craftsmen's Corner" collection, the *Peddler, Billy Bum, Nast Santa* and *Clown Girl*. Photograph courtesy of the Effanbee Doll Corporation.

7004 – ANCHORS AWEIGH – Girl

7003 – ANCHORS AWEIGH – Boy

7002 – PARTY TIME – Girl

7001
PARTY TIME
Boy

7006 – CLOWN – Girl

7005 – CLOWN – Boy

Faith Wick
Originals

From the 1980 Effanbee catalog, 16in (41cm) vinyl dolls from their "Craftsmen's Corner," *Clown Boy, Clown Girl,*

Faith Wick™ Originals

7111 — 18"
HEARTH WITCH — Soft Body

7110 — 18"
WICKET WITCH — Soft Body

From the 1982 Effanbee catalog, *Hearth Witch*
and *Wicket Witch*, both with soft bodies.

No limit was set on quantity for any of the above dolls. *Clown Girl* was one of Effanbees best sellers in 1982.

During 1978-80 Wick gave courses and demonstrations around the country in connection with her doll promotions at doll shows and before doll-oriented audiences.

"I became acquainted with Seeley's Ceramics," she says, "at the International Plate Convention in South Bend, Indiana, in 1980. We admired each other's products and shared the same ethnic background. They are interested in educating the doll makers in methods of sculpture which will enable them to make their own originals.

"Since then we have worked together on various projects including a new line of sculpture for the hobby industry: a plate, a bell, a mug, a stein and tree ornaments. All of these have the Victorian Father Christmas theme. They are sold as molds for ceramicists and are soon to be offered by Seeley Ceramics."

In June of 1983, as a result of this association, Seeley's commissioned Rolf E. Ericson and Ragnhild Ericson, photographer, to produce a highly detailed book on Faith Wick's sculpting procedure. Meticulously illustrated steps, especially in the modeling routine, make the process clear to anyone seriously interested in mastering the sculpture of a face in clay or similar materials. Instruction for boots and hands is included.

(*Sculpting Little People*. Faith Wick's Guide to basic sculpting techniques. Volume I: Grandma and Grandpa. 50 pp. 8½ x 11. By Rolf E. Ericson, published by Seeley's Ceramic Service, Inc., 9 River Street, Oneonta, N. Y. 13820.)

1979: "Todd Riddell, an owner of a manufacturers' representatives' group based in Atlanta, Miami, Dallas and Los Angeles, was my 'rep' for dolls," Faith states. "He suggested I make prototypes of dolls for Christmas decorations and send them to Silvestri. They were accepted and also I was hired by another division of their company, Balos, which produces high-style giftware."

1980: *Carolina* for Charlotte, North Carolina, Regional Convention. 150 pieces. (Companion doll: *Charles*, limit 25. Sculptured red hair. Gold, tan and brown eton suit. Produced by Toppers of Vandalia, Michigan.)

1980: U.F.D.C. Convention, St. Louis, Missouri, *Lindberg*, 21in (53cm) tall. 1200 heads. Bodies available; also aviator suit. Boots by Yvonne Parker were given as convention prize. Produced by Viv Mertins of Wisconsin.

1981: "Dollspart sent a letter to all NIADA artists and to other doll artists as well. Dollspart asked them to submit designs. They wrote me, then sent a representative to Grand Rapids. They selected a face they liked and produced the characters: *Baby Plays Mommy!*, *Baby Scarecrow*, *Baby Bunny* and *Poor Cinderella*. They were introduced in 1982." These porcelain dolls all had soft bodies and were a limited edition of 1000.

"In 1983, Dollspart produced a *Baby Clown* and a *Baby Hobo* and a *Mother* and *Child*." These were also limited to 1000 pieces.

In 1984, *Nursery Humpty*, *Nursery Queen of Hearts* and *Puss in Boots* were manufactured by Dollspart and sold by Reeves International, Inc.

Dollspart

Name	Size	Years Made
"Children's Costume Party"		
Baby Plays Mommy	18in (46cm)	1982-83
Baby Scarecrow	18in (46cm)	1982-83
Baby Bunny	18in (46cm)	1982
Baby Poor Cinderella	18in (46cm)	1982
Baby Clown	18in (46cm)	1983
Baby Hobo	18in (46cm)	1983
Mother and Child	18in (46cm) with 5in (13cm) baby	1983
Nursery Humpty	8in (20cm) seated	1984
Nursery Queen of Hearts	16in (41cm)	1984
Puss in Boots	18in (46cm)	1984

FAITHWICK™
CHILDREN'S COSTUME PARTY

Baby Plays Mommy
FW 181
18"

Baby Scarecrow
FW 182
18"

Baby Bunny
FW 183
18"

Baby Poor Cinderella
FW 184
18"

From the 1982 Dollspart catalog, the "Children's Costume Party." This series includes: *Baby Plays Mommy* in overalls, skirt, pink velour dress and feather boa, pocketbook, pearls and hat; *Baby Scarecrow* wears bright orange pants, print shirt and floppy hat and has a painted face; *Baby Bunny* is, of course, dressed in a white plush outfit with long pink ears; *Baby Poor Cinderella* in a lavender skirt, shawl and print blouse. She holds a broom. All of the dolls are 18in (46cm).

Added to the "Children's Costume Party" in 1983 were *Baby Clown* and *Baby Hobo*. 1983 Dollspart catalog.

From the 1983 Dollspart catalog, *Mother and Child*. The 18in (46cm) mother is dressed in a traditional penoir and the 5in (13cm) baby in a Christening outfit. Limited edition of 1000.

1981: Milly August, Atlanta, Georgia, Miniatures. "I sold the 'Holly Hobby' design outright for her to manufacture (under an American Greeting Card license)."

1982: "I contacted R. Dakin and Co. about wanting to do some vinyl-faced designs of animals. They were interested in that, but even more interested in developing a line of vinyl art dolls, with the concept of having dolls with real people proportions, rather than the more common exaggerated figures. This style I liked and so an arrangement was made in 1983 to design and produce a line of dolls." Work began in 1984 and Dakin began marketing these dolls in 1985.

R. Dakin & Company

Name	Size	Years Made
Pip	18in (46cm)	1985-86
Merlin	21in (53cm)	1985-86
Alice	16in (41cm)	1985-86
White Rabbit	16in (41cm)	1985-86
Mad Hatter	16in (41cm)	1985-86
Elvin	13in (33cm)	1985-86
Susanna	16in (41cm)	1985-86
Lily	16in (41cm)	1985-86
Rumpelstiltskin	12in (31cm)	1986
Miller's Daughter	22in (56cm)	1986
The Bag Lady	12in (31cm)	1986

From the R. Dakin and Company 1985 catalog, 18in (46cm) *Pip* with a crimson and black costume featuring gold lamé trim, including shoes and collar.

21in (53cm) *Merlin* in a flowing star-printed robe with gold lamé inner sleeves trimmed with fur plush by R. Dakin and Company. *Photograph courtesy of R. Dakin and Company.*

Alice, the White Rabbit *and the* Mad Hatter, *all 16in (41cm), from the well-known story. Manufactured by R. Dakin and Company.* Photograph courtesy of R. Dakin and Company.

Dakin's 16in (41cm) Susanna portraying an American pioneer woman. She wears a cotton print dress with apron, petticoat, bloomers and work boots. *Photograph courtesy of R. Dakin and Company.*

16in (41cm) *Lily*, a peddler doll with a fully-lined wool cape and lace-trimmed bonnet by R. Dakin and Company. *Photograph courtesy of R. Dakin and Company.*

13in (33cm) *Elvin* costumed with genuine leather vest, hat and boots. Manufactured by R. Dakin and Company. *Photograph courtesy of R. Dakin and Company.*

From the 1986 R. Dakin and Company catalog, the 22in (56cm) *Miller's Daughter* wearing a pink sheer fabric-draped hat and a crepe de chine dress with a purple cummerbund. Her accessories include her famous wooden spindle and gold thread.

*70-0027 MILLER'S DAUGHTER

From the 1986 R. Dakin and Company catalog, 12in (31cm) *Rumpelstiltskin* costumed in a box-pleated ultra-suede tunic, wool cape, felt elfin hat and gold leather pouch.

From the R. Dakin and Company 1986 catalog, the 12in (31cm) *Bag Lady* appropriately dressed in a camel-colored patch coat and carrying a woven bag with her treasures in it and a small print purse. Completing the outfit is a "stylish" hat.

During 1984 Faith transferred from Dollspart to Silvestri where she had been creating doll ornaments successfully for a number of years. During 1985 and 1986 Faith designed a large variety of dolls for Silvestri as well as ornaments.

Silvestri Corporation (Balos)

Name	Size	Number in Edition	Years Made
White Rabbit	30in (76cm)	750	1985-86
Alice	27½in (70cm)	2000	1985-86
Mad Hatter	31in (79cm)	750	1985-86
Duchess	27in (69cm)	750	1985-86
Cheshire Cat	25½in (65cm)	750	1985-86
Queen of Hearts	27in (69cm)	750	1985-86
Wicked Witch	29in (74cm)	1313	1986
Michael, musical playing "Cieleto Lindo"	16in (41cm)	2500	1986
Pinnochio Marionette		5000	1985-86
White Rabbit	18in (46cm)	4000	1985-86
Cheshire Cat	14in (36cm)	4000	1985-86
Alice	18in (46cm)	4000	1985-86
Mad Hatter	16in (41cm)	4000	1985-86
March Hare	18in (46cm)	4000	1985-86
Humpty Dumpty	14in (36cm)	4000	1985-86
Tweedledum	16in (41cm)	4000	1985-86
Tweedledee	16in (41cm)	4000	1985-86
Ruthie	9½in (24cm)	7500	1984-86
Richie	9½in (24cm)	7500	1984-86
Bobby	11¼in (29cm)	7500	1984-86
Big Brother	11¼in (29cm)	7500	1984
Polly	12in (31cm)	7500	1984-86
Peter	9¾in (25cm)	7500	1984-86
Valerie Valentine	13½in (34cm)	5000	1984-86
Celebration Clown	17½in (44cm)	5000	1984-86
Mother's Day	14¼in (36cm)	3000	1984-86
Hunny Bunny	19in (48cm)	7500	1984-86
Hunny Bunny	8in (30cm)	?	1984-86
Father Christmas	19in (48cm)	5000	1984
Nicholas	9¾in (25cm)	7500	1984-86
Eve	12in (31cm)	7500	1984-86
Merry	12in (31cm)	5000	1984-86
Noel	12in (31cm)	5000	1984-86
Santa Claus	20in (51cm)	3000	1984-86
Rudolph	10in (25cm)	7500	1985-86
Rimsky	10in (25cm)	7500	1985-86
Vladimir	10in (25cm)	7500	1985-86
Fillipa	19in (48cm)	5000	1985-86
Ruby	14in (36cm)	5000	1984
Rudy	14in (36cm)	5000	1984
Marottes			
Duchess		1500	1985-86
Queen of Hearts		1500	1985-86
Mad Hatter		1500	1985-86
White Rabbit		1500	1985-86
Cheshire Cat		1500	1985-86
Alice		1500	1985-86
Ivan		1500	1985-86
Filippo		1500	1985-86

The Wise Egg-head, *Humpty Dumpty*, expounding on some deep subject and expecting we will all listen and be able to understand all he says — especially when he talks about walls, horses and king's men. Manufactured by Balos, 1984. *Photograph by Pam Leenbo.*

Queen of Hearts by Balos, 1984. *Photograph by Tim Wick.*

Rimsky, Rudolph and *Valdimar* — very natural looking bears in northern Minnesota, an appropriate setting for three playful bears. Manufactured by Bålos, 1984. *Photograph by Tim Wick.*

The Cheshire Cat manufactured by Balos, 1984. *Photograph by Tim Wick.*

Silvestri Dollcrafter Classics are 30in (76cm) *White Rabbit* (edition 750), 27½in (70cm) *Alice* (edition 2000) and 31in (79cm) *Mad Hatter* (edition 750).

Two Wick marottes manufactured by Balos, 19in (48cm) *Mad Hatter* and 16in (41cm) *Queen of Hearts*. Each an edition of 1500.

Designed by Faith Wick and manufactured by Balos are *Alice Marotte*, 17½in (44cm); *Cheshire Cat Marotte*, 13in (33cm); *White Rabbit Marotte*, 17½in (44cm). *Alice* is an edition of 3000. The others are an edition of 1500.

29in (74cm) *Wicked Witch* designed by Faith Wick for Silvestri Doll
Crafter Classics, 1986. Limited
worldwide edition of 1313. *Photograph courtesy of the Silvestri
Corporation.*

Alice appearing in one of the five display windows featuring Faith Wick's dolls by Silvestri at Marshall Field & Co., Chicago, Illinois. *Photograph courtesy of the Silvestri Corporation.*

10-208
Pinnochio
Marionette
(12"—17" Stand)
edition:
5,000

Pinnochio Marionette from the 1986 Silvestri Corporation catalog.

Faith Wick's musical *Michael*, 16in (41cm) tall plays "Cieleto Lindo." *Michael* is a limited edition of 2500 by Silvestri.

80

Faith Wick dolls from the 1986 Silvestri Corporation catalog.

10-175
Richie
(9½")
edition:
7,500

10-176
Polly
(12")
edition:
7,500

10-173
Ruthie
(9½")
edition:
7,500

10-412
(plaque)

10-174
Bobby
(11¼")
edition:
7,500

10-172
Peter
(9¾")
edition:
7,500

Ruthie, Richie, Bobby, Polly and *Peter* from the 1986 Silvestri Corporation catalog.

10-180
*Valerie
Valentine*
(13½")
edition: 5,000

10-181
Mother's Day
(14¼")
edition:
3,000

10-177
Hunny Bunny
(19")
edition:
7,500

10-179
*Celebration
Clown*
(17½")
edition:
5,000

10-178
Hunny Bunny
(8")

Holiday dolls from the 1986 Silvestri Corporation catalog.

82

Merry, Noel and Santa Claus from
the 1986 Silvestri Corporation
catalog.

Faith Wick Christmas ornaments
by Silvestri, a sample of the many
Wick designs in Silvestri's Christmas collection. *Photograph courtesy of the Silvestri Corporation.*

Wick designs from the 1984 Balos catalog.

Wick designs from the 1984 Balos catalog.

Eight-piece creche set designed by Faith Wick for Silvestri's Christmas line. *Courtesy of the Silvestri Corporation.*

SILVESTRI®

1981: Faith Wick began working with Enesco Imports Corp. Her initial designs were for a series of musical, bisque boy clown dolls inspired by the work of artist Maxfield Parrish. *Pom Pom, the Clowns* were of white bisque with red trim.

Faith also designed Ye Olde Peddlers, porcelain figures based on peddlers she encountered in her youth.

Her latest venture with Enesco has been a variety of limited edition musical jack-in-the-boxes. The first issue, the Jester, playing "Memories," was selected for the honor of "Best Collectible Item for 1984" by Gifts Creations Concepts. The second issue was Jingle Bear, playing "Pachebell Canon." Issue No. 3 is Annabelle playing "Rhapsody" on a theme of Paganini. A fourth issue will be available in 1987. They all have laminated wooden boxes and hand-painted porcelain heads. Limited to 2500 each, they are numbered and come with a certificate of authenticity.

Seven new jack-in-the-boxes have been designed in 1986, to be released the following year, 7500 pieces of each. They are to be an exclusive for J. C. Penney Company, Inc. and are as follows:

Here Comes Santa Claus (playing the tune of the same name)
Monarch of the Midway Lion (playing "The Entertainer")
Grimaldi Clown (playing "Send in the Clowns")
T'was the Night Before Christmas (playing "Jolly Ole St. Nicholas")
Punchinello Puppet (playing "Concerto No. 1" by Tchaikovsky)
Ursa, the Bear (playing "Troika")
Scaramouche Jester (playing "Greensleeves")

Jester jack-in-the-box won the award of "Best Collectible Item for 1984" by Gifts Creations Concepts. The limited edition of 2500 plays "Memories." *Photograph courtesy of Enesco Imports Corp.*

Jingle Bear jack-in-the-box, Issue No. 2 for Enesco plays "Pachebell Canon." The bear wears a navy blue hat trailing a bell and slender streamers of white, blue and brown ribbons. His ruffled collar is navy, gray and blue. Limited edition of 2500. *Photograph courtesy of Enesco Imports Corp.*

Here Comes Santa Claus jack-in-the-box which plays the tune of the same name. *Photograph courtesy of Enesco Imports Corp.*

Monarch of the Midway Lion jack-in-the-box which plays "The Entertainer." *Photograph courtesy of Enesco Imports Corp.*

Grimaldi Clown jack-in-the-box which plays "Send in the Clowns." *Photograph courtesy of Enesco Imports Corp.*

T'was the Night Before Christmas jack-in-the-box which plays "Jolly Ole St. Nicholas." *Photograph courtesy of Enesco Imports Corp.*

Punchinello Puppet jack-in-the-box which plays "Concerto No. 1" by Tchaikovsky. *Photograph courtesy of Enesco Imports Corp.*

Ursa, the Bear jack-in-the-box which plays "Troika." *Photograph courtesy of Enesco Imports Corp.*

Scaramouche Jester jack-in-the-box which plays "Greensleeves." *Photograph courtesy of Enesco Imports Corp.*

1986: Faith has signed a contract with Cal-Star of Minneapolis, Minnesota, to create a line of fine figurines for sale through direct mail.

All these design contracts, while highly successful, became more and more time-consuming. Faith and Mel were constantly rearranging their big old house as one after another the children departed for college and careers and homes of their own. Even a separate house for the large doll collection and doll work proved less than adequate.

They had to rethink the whole doll operation and figure a better system.

In order for Faith to have a quiet time for herself, she and Melvin have a Florida condominium where she does much of her sculpting.

VI.
New House and
New Plans

"We decided to sell our Grand Rapids home and the "doll house." The spot we loved best was the wooded one overlooking the Mississippi River where we had spent so many happy summers in the little A-frame house. We selected that site. The 'two big barns connected by a silo are postal blue with white trim and are called 'Blue Barns of Bass Brook' — very Scandinavian."

Dolls are everywhere. In a large room above the garage with a separate staircase leading up to it are banks of glass cases on which are displayed the 600 prototypes Wick designed for the Wicket Originals, as well as numerous dolls from Wick's collection. Dolls are arranged in wall cabinets or posed in groups in the other rooms, too.

The living room contains the only piano, a concert grand, with nearby an obvious bow to Wick's love of the theatrical — a red satin sofa called "Marilyn," which is a giant sensuous pair of lips.

The kitchen-dining room has a farm theme and a long view of the Mississippi River through its bank of windows. From the balcony just outside this room one can come even closer to the river and see nearly a quarter-mile of it.

On the lower floor, the large dormitory has a Scandinavian theme including a cedar-lined sauna, while the luxurious master bedroom is oriental in feeling and design with touches of Art Deco.

The architect has a fine regional reputation and he enjoyed working out the design of the rather complicated house. One day he brought a friend who is a decorator with a national reputation to look at the half-finished house. The decorator was enchanted. He said, "Let me do the decorating." Faith said, "We can't afford you." "Sure, you can," he said, "I'll take a couple of dolls in trade."

He is doing a marvelous job. It may even be flamboyant enough to suit Faith's love of drama.

This home won the prestigious Architecture Minnesota (AM) Award for 1985 as "House of the Year."

Mel is doing all the custom finishing of the interior. It is work he loves to do and there is no skimping on materials or craftsmanship.

At this writing there is the possibility of the opening of three museums in different parts of the country, exhibiting most of the dolls listed in this book. The dolls have been collected by three gentlemen over a period of many years. Each museum would reflect a different segment of Faith Wick's work.

Heidi with Grandma, Faith Wick's mother.

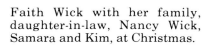

Faith Wick with her family, daughter-in-law, Nancy Wick, Samara and Kim, at Christmas.

Faith Wick with her eldest daughter, Kim, and granddaughter, Samara.

Elfie.